French

Vicky Taithe

**Age 9–11
Years 5–6**
Key Stage 2

Advice for parents

This book is designed for children to practise and consolidate their learning in line with the new National Curriculum and has been written by a practising primary class teacher with experience of teaching languages across Key Stage 2. Some of the language contained in this book will be familiar to your child, while other topic areas or aspects of grammar may be new to them. This will depend on the scheme of work followed by your child's school and how much time your child has already spent learning French.

The vocabulary used to explain the French grammar is the same as that used in teaching English grammar in the new National Curriculum, so your child should have come across all the terms used in this book. Moreover, encountering these terms again while learning French will help children recall their English grammar learning and appreciate how this can help them to learn other languages.

Language learning consists of mastering the four skills of listening, speaking, reading and writing, generally in that order. This book necessarily focuses on reading and writing correctly, which in turn will help children to improve their general understanding and accuracy in listening and speaking. Another aspect of primary language learning that this book includes is that of intercultural understanding, highlighting interesting similarities and differences between our languages and customs.

Discuss with your children what they have learned already and what they can do independently. If they come across any unfamiliar words, it is good to practise using a dictionary, whether in book form or online.

- The **Get ready** section introduces the new learning points and sets them in context.
- The **Let's practise** section helps to consolidate and check understanding.
- **Have a go** provides an opportunity to be more adventurous, extend sentence writing or try something new.
- **Teacher's tips** are self-explanatory, clarifying tricky or surprising facts about French language and culture.
- The **Language tools** and **Glossary** are at the back, but it is useful to have a quick look at these early on.
- **How have I done?** is a type of self-assessment exercise with which many children are already familiar. It should help children to feel good about what they have learned and to identify their next steps.

Audio downloads of key words and phrases are available at: www.whsmith.co.uk/readytoprogress

Hachette UK's policy is to use papers that are natural, renewable and recyclable products and made from wood grown in sustainable forests. The logging and manufacturing processes are expected to conform to the environmental regulations of the country of origin.

Orders: you can order online or find your local WHSmith store at: www.whsmith.co.uk

© Vicky Taithe 2014
First published in 2014 exclusively for WHSmith by
Hodder Education
An Hachette UK Company
338 Euston Road
London NW1 3BH

Impression number   10 9 8 7 6 5 4 3 2 1
Year   2018 2017 2016 2015 2014

Cover illustration by Oxford Designers and Illustrators Ltd.
Illustrations by Redmoor Design
Character illustrations: Beehive illustration
Typeset in Folio by Aptara®, Inc.
Printed in Italy

A catalogue record for this title is available from the British Library

ISBN 978 1 4718 3543 8

"

Contents

Welcome to Kids Club! 4

1 Who's who? 6

2 Hello! How are you? 8

3 How old are you? 10

4 What colour is it? 12

5 Where do you live? 14

6 Do you have a pet? 16

7 At home 18

8 Sport and music 20

9 How to be positive or negative 22

10 The week at school 24

11 What's the date today? 26

12 Special days 28

13 What is the weather like today? 30

14 I am putting on my shirt 32

15 Head, shoulders, knees and feet! 34

16 Meal times 36

17 What do I do now? 38

18 It's holiday time! 40

How have I done? 42

Answers 43

Language tools 47

Welcome to Kids Club!

I'm Abbie. Let's meet the kids who will work with you on the activities in this book.

Hi, I'm Megan. I've made friends with all the kids at Kids Club. I like the outings and trips we go on the best.

I'm Amina. I like to do my homework at Kids Club. Charlie and Abbie are always very helpful. We're like one big happy family.

Now you've met us all, tell us something about yourself. All the kids filled in a '**Personal Profile**' when they joined. Here's one for you to complete.

Personal profile

INSERT PHOTO OF YOURSELF HERE

Name: _______________________________________

Age: _______

School: _____________________________________

Home town: _________________________________

I have been learning French since _________________________

I have spoken French in _______________________________

I can also speak _____________________________

My favourite word:

- in English is ____________________.

- in French is ____________________.

- in any language is ____________.

My international hero is _____________________________ because

____.

When I grow up I want to be a _______________________________.

It will be useful to me to understand different languages because ____

____.

If I could travel to anywhere in the world for a day, I would go to

____

____.

1: Who's who?

Bonjour! We have friends in many French-speaking parts of the world and we would like you to meet some of them. Read their introductions in French and draw a line to match them up to the English translation, then fill in their name.

Bonjour! Je m'appelle Mathilde. J'habite à Paris, la capitale de la France.

1 Hello! I am called ________________. I live in Marseille in the south of France.

Bonjour! Mon nom est Louis. J'habite à Nouméa en Nouvelle Calédonie. C'est sur une île dans l'océan Pacifique.

2 Hi! I am ________________. I live in Montreal in Quebec. It's in Canada.

Salut! Je suis Céline. J'habite à Montréal au Québec. C'est au Canada.

3 Hello! My name is ________________. I live in Nouméa in New Caledonia. It's on an island in the Pacific Ocean.

Bonjour! Je m'appelle Naeem. J'habite à Marseille dans le sud de la France.

Hello! I am called Mathilde. I live in Paris, the capital city of France.

Qui est qui?

Now let's complete the introductions of our Kids Club friends.

Salut les lecteurs. Mon nom est Charlie.

1  Salut. _________ suis Megan. Tous les enfants à Kids Club sont mes amis.

2  Mon nom est ________________. J'aime le sport.

3  Bonjour, mon nom ________ Kim. Kids Club est super cool.

4 Salutations les lecteurs. Je m' ________________ Alfie. On va s'amuser!

Work out how to introduce yourself in French to a new friend. Where might this be useful? Find out where in the world French is spoken. In an atlas or using maps on the internet, locate the homes of Mathilde, Naeem, Céline and Louis.

____

____

Teacher's tips

Careful reading involves spotting patterns in the sentences and looking for clues. The sentences in French on page 6 provide models for completing those on page 7.

Bonjour! It's good to check out how your friends are feeling and to know how to answer the question **ça va?** If they ask first, remember you can return the question to them by asking, **Et toi?**

 ## Get ready

Of course, there are lots of ways to answer this question **ça va?** So here are some useful ones.

Ça va très bien.

Ça va bien.

Ça va.

Comme-ci comme-ça.

Ça ne va pas.

Ça va mal.

Ça va très mal.

Read the question that Mathilde is asking you and reply in French.

Let's practise

Kim has received this email from Naeem, who is happy to be his new penfriend. Read it carefully and help to complete his reply.

Naeem naeem@kidsclub.fr
To: Kim

Bonjour!

Je m'appelle Naeem.  Ça va très bien. Je suis content de t'écrire par mail.

Et toi, ça va?

Salut!
Naeem

Have a go

Kim kim@kidsclub.uk
À: Naeem

____

____

____

À bientôt. (Let's write again soon.)
Kim

Teacher's tips

The word 'ça' is pronounced with a soft 's' sound. Without the cedilla under the c, this would be said as a hard 'c' as in 'car'. C is also pronounced with a soft 's' sound when followed by e or i, as in 'cinéma' and 'pièce'. As in English, all sentences begin with a capital letter. Capital letters are sometimes written without accents.

There is more than one way to ask some questions, so you may have seen one or both of the French ways before. To ask and answer this question correctly, it is helpful to know that the verb used in this sentence is the verb **avoir** – to have. So we are literally saying: What age do you 'have'? And we reply: J'ai neuf ans – I 'have' nine years.

As in English, the subject of the sentence and the verb must agree. Let's look at how verbs change according to the subject of the sentence.

To have	Avoir
I have	J'ai
You have	Tu as
He has She has It has	Il a Elle a Il a/Elle a – *depends on noun gender*
We have	Nous avons
You have (*plural or/and respectful*)	Vous avez
They have	Ils ont Elles ont

Get ready

Quel âge as-tu?

Complete these translations.

Bonjour! Je m'appelle Mathilde. J'ai neuf ans.

Hello! I am called Mathilde. I am nine years old.

1 Salut! Mon nom est Louis. J'ai dix ans.

   Hi! My name is Louis. I am _______________________________.

2 Bonjour! Je suis Céline. J'ai onze ans.

   Hello! I am Céline. I _______________________________.

 **Let's practise**

Now let's continue our introductions of our Kids Club friends. Fill in the gaps.

C'est qui? Quel âge a-t-il?

Voici Naeem. **Il a dix ans.**

1. C'est qui? Quel âge a-t-il?

Voici Alfie. __________________ __________________. (9)

2. C'est qui? Quel âge a-t-elle?

Voici Jamelia. Elle __________ __________________. (9)

3. C'est qui? Quel âge a-t-elle?

Voici Megan. ______________ __________________. (10)

4. C'est qui? Quel âge ont-ils?

Voici Alfie et Jamelia. Ils ont __________________. (9)

5. C'est qui? Quel âge ont-ils?

Voici Megan et Naeem. ______ __________________. (10)

Have a go

Work out how to introduce yourself in French giving your age. Which of your friends could you also introduce?

____

Teacher's tips

Practise spelling numbers up to eleven:

un   deux   trois   quatre   cinq   six   sept   huit   neuf   dix   onze

These numbers in French include lots of different and useful phonemes that occur in many other words. Learning these will help you to work out other spellings.

Dans un arc-en-ciel on trouve ces sept couleurs:

rouge, orange, jaune, vert, bleu, bleu foncé et violet.

Get ready

You probably also know: blanc, noir, gris, rose, marron ou brun.

To say the colour is dark, add **foncé** – bleu foncé, vert foncé.

Or for light shades, add **clair** – bleu clair, vert clair.

Let's look at another very useful verb now: to be – **être**. Try to learn how it changes too.

To be	Etre
I am	Je suis
You are	Tu es
He is She is It is	Il est Elle est Il est/Elle est
We are	Nous sommes
You are (*plural or/and respectful*)	Vous êtes
They are	Ils sont Elles sont

C'est de quelle couleur?

Let's practise

Now draw some mini-monsters and colour them according to the description.

1

2

Have a go

Invent your own mini-monster and complete the sentences to describe it.

Voici mon mini-monstre.

Il s'appelle _________________. (Name)

Il a _______________. (Age)

Il est _______________. (Colour)

Teacher's tips

All French nouns have a gender – either masculine or feminine. This is explained further on the next page. For now just remember that monsters are always masculine in French, so the pronoun **it** must be translated as **il**, meaning 'he' or 'it' when replacing a masculine noun.

How do you begin your answer to this question? Look back to page 6 and spot the phrase 'J'habite' in the French-speaking friends' introductions.

To live – **habiter** is a regular verb. This means that its spelling changes according to the same pattern as lots of other verbs.

To live	Habiter
I live	J'habite
You live	Tu habites
He lives She lives It lives	Il habite Elle habite Il habite/Elle habite
We live	Nous habitons
You live (*plural or/and respectful*)	Vous habitez
They live	Ils habitent Elles habitent

Get ready

Fill the gaps with the right form of the verb to complete the sentences about our Kids Club friends.

1. Je suis Mathilde. J' _________________ à Paris.

2. Il est Louis. Il _________________ à Nouméa.

3. Elle est Céline. Elle _________________ au Canada.

4. Il est Naeem. Il _________________ en France.

5. Nous sommes Charlie et Abbie. Nous _________________ à Londres.

6. Elles sont Megan et Amina. Elles _________________ en Angleterre.

Où habites-tu?

We can also say more about our homes. Do we live in a flat (un appartement) or a house (une maison)?

Where is our home? In a town or city (en ville), in the countryside (à la campagne), by the sea (au bord de la mer) or in the hills or mountains (à la montagne)?

Céline habite dans un appartement en ville.

Louis habite dans une maison au bord de la mer.

Look back to page 6 and use your detective skills to work out how you could describe the homes of Mathilde and Naeem.

Mathilde ____.

Naeem ____.

What is the fullest answer you could now give to the question:
Où habites-tu?

J' ____

____

____

____

Teacher's tips

When 'h' is the first letter of a word in French, it is generally a silent letter. The first phoneme (sound) we hear in *habiter* is *a*. This is why the *e* of 'je' is omitted and replaced by an apostrophe to form *j'habite*. This happens every time *je, ce, le, que, ne* are followed by a word beginning with a vowel or a silent *h*.

6: Do you have a pet?

The words animal, cat, dog, rabbit and tortoise are all nouns. This means that, because all French nouns have a gender (masculine or feminine), when you learn the words, you also need to learn the gender. In most dictionaries a masculine noun is followed by *nm* and a feminine by *nf*.

You may also find *nmpl* and *nfpl*. Can you work out what these mean?

In French, determiners (words such as a, an, the – **un**, **une**, **le**, **la**) vary according to the gender of the noun. Look out for *des* and *les* before plural nouns.

Get ready

Let's build up some sentences about animals. Fill in the gaps.

le chat *nm*

Le chat habite dans un appartement.

J'ai un chat. Il est noir et blanc.

le chien *nm*

1 Le _______ habite dans une maison à la montagne.

Alfie a _______ chien.
Il _______ marron.

le lapin *nm*

2 Le lapin ___________ dans un jardin.

Elle _______ un lapin.
Il _______ noir.

Most are masculine nouns but a few are feminine.

la tortue *nf*

3 La tortue ___________ à la campagne.

J'ai une tortue. Elle s' ___________ Fred.

As-tu un animal?

As-tu un animal? Tu as un animal?

Do you have a pet? Do you have any animals?

Our questions include the verb to have – **avoir**, so have a quick look back at this on page 10.

Now match up the pictures to the descriptions and colour them in correctly.

1 J'ai un chien rouge.

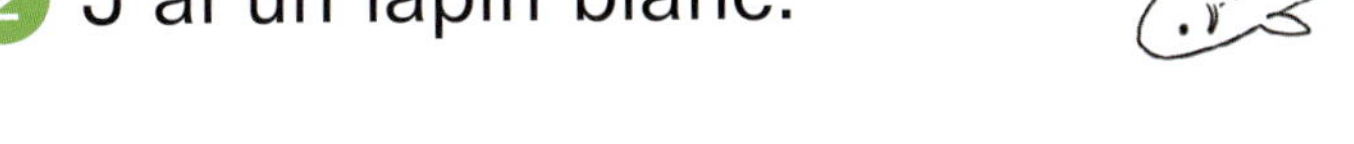

2 J'ai un lapin blanc.

3 J'ai un poisson rouge.*

4 J'ai un chat gris.

5 J'ai une tortue jaune.

*Un poisson rouge (a red fish) is a goldfish too.

Have a go

Draw your dream pet and have a go at describing it. Use the sentence models to help you.

J'ai un _______________________________

Teacher's tips

Playing with language is fun and an important part of the learning process. Imitate sentences that you have read and change a few of the words to make your own ones. You could also look up the names of other animals in a dictionary.

We used the word **maison** on page 15 to mean house but you need to know that it can also mean home. The phrase **à la maison** means both 'at the house' and 'at home'.

The little word **à**, like *at* in English, is a preposition. Prepositions are words that tell you where things and people are in relation to each other or where they are moving to.

in – dans 

on – sur 

Get ready

Now draw your own diagrams for these prepositions.

under – sous

next to – à côté de 

in front of – devant 

with – avec

behind – derrière 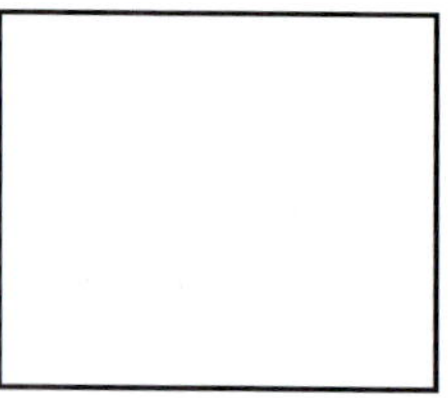

À la maison

Let's practise

Read the following sentences and underline the prepositions in each sentence.

Céline est <u>à</u> la maison <u>avec</u> son chat.

1. Charlie est dans le jardin devant la maison.

2. Le lapin est derrière la maison.

3. La tortue est sous sa maison.

4. Naeem habite dans un appartement à côté de la mer.

Have a go

Complete these sentences by adding suitable prepositions from the list on page 18.

1. Je suis _______________ la maison* _______________ mon chat.

2. Le chat est _______________ le lit (bed) _______________ ma chambre.

3. Le chien est _______________ le jardin _______________ la maison.

*Another way of saying 'I am at home' is: **Je suis chez moi**.

8: Sport and music

When you are making friends it is good to find out what they like doing and to share with them what you like doing too.

Qu'est-ce que tu fais pour rester en forme?

What do you do to stay fit is a useful question to ask and of course there are lots of possible answers. You should be able to match up most of the possible French answers to the English equivalent. There are some tricky ones that you just have to learn!

Get ready

Draw a line to match each activity to its translation.

1. Je joue au foot.
2. Je fais du vélo.
3. Je joue au tennis.
4. Je fais de la danse.
5. Je fais du skate.
6. Je fais de la natation.

 I skateboard.

 I dance.

 I play tennis.

 I play football.

 I swim.

I ride my bike.

You could also ask your friend if they play a musical instrument.

Qu'est-ce que tu joues? If the instrument is a masculine noun, the reply begins: Je joue du… and if it is feminine, it begins: Je joue de la… .

Qu'est-ce que tu joues?

Je joue du piano et du violon.

Je joue de la guitare, de la clarinette, de la trompette et de la batterie.

Most instrument names are very similar to the English words – except for la batterie, which isn't a battery but drums, which you beat or batter!

Le sport et la musique

Let's practise

How would each of these kids answer the questions in a role play?
Write their replies, using the sentences on page 20 to help you.

1 Abbie: Salut, Charlie! Qu'est-ce que tu fais pour rester en forme?

Charlie: ____

(football).

2 Abbie: Salut, Jamelia! Qu'est-ce que tu fais pour rester en forme?

Jamelia: ____

(dance).

3 Abbie: Salut, Amina! Qu'est-ce que tu joues?

Amina: ____

(piano).

4 Abbie: Salut, Kim! Qu'est-ce que tu joues?

Kim: ____

(drums).

Have a go

Now it's your turn. Have a go at answering the questions yourself –
your answers don't have to be completely truthful for this exercise
but try to copy the spellings carefully.

Qu'est-ce que tu fais pour rester en forme?

Je ____.

Qu'est-ce que tu joues?

Je joue ____

Teacher's tips

If your favourite sport or instrument is not included in these pages, try to look it up in
a French dictionary, or type 'French dictionary' in a web browser. Remember to write
down the gender (*nm* or *nf*) so you know whether to write *du* or *de la*.

9: How to be positive or negative

At Kids Club we like to be positive and have a go at all the challenges that come our way. We like to say: Oui!

As in Maths and Science, though, we need to learn about negatives in language. Sometimes we need to express our feelings about what we like or dislike.

Here are some useful phrases to explain how much you do or don't like something.

 J'adore

J'aime beaucoup

J'aime

Je n'aime pas

Je n'aime pas du tout

Je déteste

Get ready

Read these sentences carefully and draw a line to match each to its translation.

1	J'adore le foot.	I like dancing very much.
2	J'aime le vélo.	I love football.
3	Je n'aime pas le tennis.	I don't like skateboarding at all.
4	J'aime beaucoup la danse.	I don't like tennis.
5	Je n'aime pas du tout le skate.	I hate swimming.
6	Je déteste la natation.	I like riding my bike.

Sentences that include **ne ___ pas** are negative; like sentences in English that include *not* or *n't*.

Let's practise

Here are pairs of positive and negative sentences. Look at the language patterns and complete those with gaps.

J'aime le tennis.   Je n'aime pas le tennis.

1. J'aime le sport.   Je n'aime ________ le ____________.

2. J'aime la clarinette.   Je ____ aime ________ la clarinette.

3. J' ________ la musique.   Je n'aime pas ______________.

Have a go

C'est à toi… It's your turn…. If a new French-speaking friend asked you what you like, how could you tell them?

Qu'est-ce que tu aimes?

J'aime ____.

Qu'est-ce que tu n'aimes pas?

Je ____.

Teacher's tips

You may also have come across another way of expressing likes and dislikes: **J'aime** or **Je n'aime pas** followed by an *infinitive verb*.

Qu'est-ce que tu aimes faire? – What do you like doing? **J'aime <u>lire</u>.** – I like reading. **Je n'aime pas du tout <u>danser</u>.** – I don't like dancing at all.

10: The week at school

Weekly timetables vary a lot in all schools. Mathilde has sent us her Year 5/6 timetable from her school in Paris. Be a good language detective and try to work out what her school week is like and think about how it compares to yours.

Mathilde: Voici l'emploi du temps de mon école primaire.

Emploi du temps – CM1 CM2					
	lundi	**mardi**	**mercredi**	**jeudi**	**vendredi**
08h30	Lecture	Lecture		Lecture – Anglais	Lecture
08h50	Mathématiques	Mathématiques		Mathématiques	Mathématiques
10h15	*Récréation*				
10h30	Français	Français		Français	Géographie
11h30	*Repas – déjeuner*				
13h30	Musique Art visuel	EPS		Instruction civique	EPS
15h15	*Récréation*				
15h30	Histoire	Anglais		Sciences	Français
16h30					

Get ready

1. On which week day doesn't she go to school? ______________

2. Each day she has a lesson in which two subjects? ______________
____

3. What foreign language does she learn? ______________

4. How many times a week does she do PE (**EPS**)? ______________

5. How long is Mathilde's lunch break? ______________

6. What is different about her reading (**Lecture**) session on Thursday?
____

La semaine à l'école

Let's practise

Qu'est-ce qu'elle fait à l'école?

What does she do at school? Check Mathilde's timetable and complete the sentences with the day of the week on which she has a lesson (**un cours**).

Lundi à 15h30 elle a un cours d'histoire.

1. ________________ à 10h30 elle a un cours de Géographie.

2. ________________ elle ne va pas à l'école.

3. ________________ à 15h30 elle a un cours de Sciences.

4. ________________ et ________________ à 13h30 elle a des cours d'EPS.

Have a go

Quelle heure est-il? What time is it?

Match and copy the time in words.

Tip: 5 is quite tricky so check the clock on page 48.

08h30 – Il est huit heures et demie.

1. 09h00 – Il est ________________
   ____

2. 10h30 – Il ________________
   ____

3. 13h30 – ________________
   ____

4. 15h15 – ________________
   ____

5. 15h45 – ________________
   ____

Il est huit heures et demie.
Il est neuf heures.
Il est dix heures et demie.
Il est une heure et demie.
Il est trois heures et quart.
Il est quatre heures moins le quart.
Il est quatre heures et demie.

Teacher's tips

The 24-hour clock is used very widely in French. Notice how the hours and minutes are separated by an **h** for **heures** in French where we would use a colon in English. RE is not taught in French state schools.

11: What's the date today?

To understand dates we need to know numbers up to 31. Let's work out some strategies for learning them.

11–16 all end in **–ze**: onze, douze, treize, quatorze, quinze, seize

17–19 all begin **dix-**: dix-sept, dix-huit, dix-neuf

20–29 all begin **vingt**: vingt, vingt et un, vingt-deux, vingt-trois, vingt-quatre, vingt-cinq, vingt-six, vingt-sept, vingt-huit, vingt-neuf

30 is **trente** and **31** is **trente et un** (thirty and one, just like 21).

Get ready

Complete these calculations in words, copying the spelling of the numbers really carefully.

neuf + trois = <u>douze</u>

1. huit + six = _______________

2. dix-neuf – quatre = _______________

3. vingt – trois = _______________

4. trois x sept = _______________

5. cinq x cinq = _______________

6. vingt-sept ÷ neuf = _______________

7. trente ÷ six = _______________

We also need to learn the months of the year – les mois de l'année. Copy.

janvier _______________   juillet _______________

février _______________   août _______________

mars _______________   septembre _______________

avril _______________   octobre _______________

mai _______________   novembre _______________

juin _______________   décembre _______________

Quelle est la date aujourd'hui?

Let's practise

Quelle est la date de ton anniversaire?

Match the answers to the calendar page.

1. Mon anniversaire c'est le 7 février.
2. Mon anniversaire c'est le 17 mars.
3. Mon anniversaire c'est le 26 juin.
4. Mon anniversaire c'est le 30 août.

26/06

30/08

17/03

07/02

Have a go

You may have learnt the rhyme 'Thirty days has September'. In French primary schools children learn poems by heart, practise for homework and then recite them in class. Have a go at learning the French version of the rhyme to learn the numbers of days in a month.

Il y a trente jours dans le mois de septembre,
Trente jours en avril,
En juin et en novembre.
Et tous les autres mois
Comptent trente et un jours.
Seul février en a vingt-huit,
Mais pas toujours.
Ce mois difficile
Il compte vingt-neuf jours
Les années bissextiles.

Teacher's tips

Just like English sentences, all French sentences begin with a capital letter, as do proper nouns, which are the names of people and places. Unlike English, days of the week and months of the year do not start with a capital letter in French, unless they are at the beginning of a sentence.

12: Special days

Every day is a special day for someone in the French-speaking world (le monde francophone). In addition to New Year's Day, Easter, Christmas, etc., names are attached to specific dates or saints' days on a French calendar. We are used to seeing (Saint) Valentine's day and Saint George's day on our calendars but in France there are many more. If you meet someone called George on 23 April, you should say, '**Bonne fête**!'

Get ready

Draw a line to match each special date to the greeting you could use on the day.

C'est le 1er janvier ___________________ Bonne année

1. C'est le 1er avril. Joyeux Noël.

2. C'est le dimanche de Pâques. Bonne fête, Émilie!

3. C'est le 19 septembre, Sainte Émilie. Joyeuses Pâques

4. C'est Noël, le 25 décembre. Poisson d'avril!*

*On April Fool's Day children often cut out paper fish and stick them on each other's backs and say, 'Poisson d'avril!'

Some other special days are public holidays in the French year:

Le 1er mai est la Fête du Travail. Workers' day when people give a lily of the valley flower – *le muguet*.

Le 14 juillet est la Fête Nationale. Bastille Day when the French Revolution is commemorated with firework displays.

Le 11 novembre et le 8 mai. The ends of the First and Second World Wars are remembered.

Le 1er novembre est la Toussaint. All Saints' or All Hallows Day. Hallowe'en is the day before.

Let's practise

We also find the first days of each season marked on some calendars.

Draw a picture for each season: spring – le printemps; summer – l'été; autumn – l'automne; winter – l'hiver.

C'est **le printemps** du 21 mars au 20 juin.

C'est **l'été** du 21 juin au 20 septembre.

C'est **l'automne** du 21 septembre au 20 décembre.

C'est **l'hiver** du 21 décembre au 20 mars.

Have a go

1st/first in French is 1er/premier – as in Premier League sport. Complete these sentences.

1. Le premier jour du printemps est le ________________________.
2. Le premier jour de l'été est le ________________________.
3. Le premier jour de l'automne ________________________.
4. Le premier jour de l' ________________________.

Teacher's tips

Une fête is a celebration, a festival or a feast day. It can also mean a party. **On va faire la fête** – if a friend says that to you, it means that you are going to have a party or have fun celebrating. The word fête is sometimes used in English for a fundraising event or fair. In French this is called **une kermesse** – not une fête!

As you learn the French phrases for describing the weather, it's great to mime what the weather is like. It helps you to remember what each means.

Il fait beau.   Thumbs up and a big smile.  The weather is fine.

Il fait mauvais.   Thumbs down and glum expression.   It's bad weather.

Il y a du soleil.   Look up, smiling and squinting.   It's sunny.

How could you mime these? Write it down in English.

Il fait chaud. _________________________________ It's hot.

Il fait froid. _________________________________ It's cold.

Il pleut. _________________________________ It's raining.

Il neige. _________________________________ It's snowing.

Get ready

Draw a calligram for each of the following. Copy the sentence so that its meaning is clear, e.g. make the **o** in *soleil* look like the sun.

Il y a du soleil.

Il pleut.

Il fait chaud.

Il fait froid.

Quel temps fait-il aujourd'hui?

Let's practise

To ask about the weather in a particular place we use the preposition **à**. Now let's find out about the weather where our friends live.

Look at the examples and complete the sentences:

Bonjour Mathilde! Quel temps fait-il à Paris?

Mathilde: Il fait 21°C. Il fait beau à Paris.

Bonjour Louis! Quel temps fait-il à Nouméa?

Louis:

1 Il fait 35°C. Il fait _______________ à Nouméa.

2 Bonjour Céline! _______________ temps fait-il à Montréal?

Céline:

3 Il fait −15°C. Il fait très _______________.

4 Bonjour Naeem! Quel _________________________ _______ à Marseille?

Naeem:

5 Il fait 26°C. _______________ du soleil à Marseille.

Have a go

Make up the weather forecast for the weekend. Draw weather symbols for each day.

Vendredi, il fait chaud. Il fait 25°C.

1 Samedi, il _______________________________.

2 Dimanche, _______________________________.

Teacher's tips

Mimes, rhymes and songs are great for making language memorable. Keep practising and sing the songs you learn in school at home. Why not try to teach French to someone at home?

14: I am putting on my shirt

Many traditional European stories, rhymes and songs include a big, bad wolf. Some are the same or similar in French and English: Little Red Riding Hood, *le petit chaperon rouge*, is originally a traditional French story, whereas 'What's the time, Mr Wolf?' is quite different: *Un, deux, trois, soleil!* (1, 2 ,3, sun!).

Here is a traditional song about going for a walk in the woods, which is safe … until the wolf has finished getting dressed. A group sings the chorus – *refrain* – while one person sings the wolf's response, saying what he is putting on next, '**Je mets…**'.

(Le refrain)

> Promenons-nous dans les bois,
> Tant que le loup n'y est pas.
> Si le loup y était
> Il nous mangerait,
> Mais comme il y est pas,
> Il nous mangera pas.
> Loup, y es-tu? Que fais-tu?
> M'entends-tu?

> Le loup: 'Je mets ma chemise.'
> (Au refrain)
> Le loup: 'Je mets ma culotte.'
> (Au refrain)
> Le loup: 'Je mets mes chaussettes.'
> (Au refrain)
> Le loup: 'Je mets ma veste.'
> (Au refrain)
> Le loup: 'Je mets mes bottes.'
> (Au refrain)
> Le loup: 'Je mets mon chapeau et j'arrive.'
> Sauvon-nous!

(*Translation on page 45*)

Get ready

Look at the wolf's replies (Le loup:). Each of the three little words beginning with **m** that follow '**Je mets**' (I am putting on or I put on) is the determiner **my**.

For masculine nouns **my** translates as   **mon**

For feminine nouns   **ma**

And for plural nouns   **mes**

Underline or highlight each of these words in the song.

Je mets ma chemise

Can you work out which of the items of clothing are plural, and whether the singular items are masculine or feminine nouns? Complete the vocabulary list.

Trousers	mon pantalon	<u>singular</u>	<u>masculine</u>	<u>nm</u>
1 Shirt	ma chemise	________	________	________
2 Socks	mes chaussettes	________	________	________
3 Hat	mon chapeau	________	________	________

Let's practise

Here are some more things you could wear in different weather.

Shorts – mon short (sing. nm)

Jacket – ma veste (sing. nf)

Dress – ma robe (sing. nf)

Coat – mon manteau (sing. nm)

Gloves – mes gants (pl. nm)

Jumper – mon pull (sing. nm)

Imitate the model to complete the sentences, choosing what to wear when the weather changes. Extra challenge: have a go and expand the noun phrase with a colour adjective after the noun.

Quant il fait beau, je mets ma chemise jaune.

(When it's fine, I put on my yellow shirt.)

1 Quand il fait froid, je mets mes ________________________ s.

2 Quand il fait mauvais, je mets m ________________________.

3 Quand il fait chaud, je ________________________.

Have a go

Learning a song helps you to remember the gender of nouns. There are lots of versions of this song available on the internet. With adult permission, search and listen to *Promenons-nous dans les bois* and try to learn it.

Teacher's tips

The determiners your – *ton, ta, tes* and his/her – *son, sa, ses* follow the same pattern as my – *mon, ma, mes*. The spelling of our – *notre* and your – *votre* (plural or polite form of you) does not vary before singular nouns but they become *nos* and *vos* in front of plurals.

At Kids Club we love singing. So stand up and sing 'Head, shoulders, knees and feet' in English. You are probably used to singing 'toes' at the end of this line, but toes in French are *les orteils* or *les doigts de pied* (literally foot fingers) and this does not scan well into the song.

Excellent! Now try this in French. It's the same sequence as in English.

La tête, les épaules, les genoux et les pieds	*Head, shoulders, knees and feet*
La tête, les épaules, les genoux et les pieds	*Head, shoulders, knees and feet*
Les yeux, les oreilles, la bouche et le nez	*Eyes, ears, mouth and nose*
La tête, les épaules, les genoux et les pieds	*Head, shoulders, knees and feet*

The names of the different parts of the body are nouns. As explained on page 16, nouns in French (as in many other languages) have a gender. They are either masculine or feminine. The determiner *the* is written in French as **le** before a masculine noun, **la** before a feminine noun or **l'** if the noun begins with a vowel or a silent h. Before a plural noun (when there are two or more – e.g. shoulders) the word to use is **les**.

Now have a look at the spelling of the endings of the plural nouns. You can spot the plural nouns because they follow the plural determiner **les**.

Make a list: ___________________

____

____

As in English, most plural nouns end with s. For example: singular (sing.) – shoulder/épaule; plural (pl.) – shoulders/épaules. Also as in English we have to learn some exceptions, e.g. foot (sing.), feet (pl.) or in French, genou (sing.), genoux (pl.).

Get ready

Draw a new mini-monster in the box
below and label different parts of its body.

La tête

Let's practise

Now colour in your mini-monster according to this description.

Il a la tête rouge, les pieds verts, les yeux bleus, la bouche jaune
et le nez orange.

Have a go

Now make up a description for a new mini-monster.

Voici mon nouveau mini-monstre. Il s'appelle _______________.

Il a ____

____.

Teacher's tips

What do you notice about the position of the colour adjectives in the description? **Il a
une tête rouge**. He has a red head. Did you notice that the adjectives describing
the plural nouns end in **s**?

16: Meal times

À table! Not a table but **à table** – to the table is an instruction called out in many French-speaking homes around the world every time a meal – **un repas** – is ready. What do you know about French meals? Did you know that French lunches and dinners have three or four courses: **l'entrée** – the starter, **le plat** – the main course, **le fromage** – the cheese, and **le dessert** – the sweet or pudding?

Kids Club asked Mathilde about her routines and meal times. Here is her reply about her day. Read it carefully and draw the hands on the clock faces.

Chers amis,

Voici ma journée (mardi et vendredi).

Le matin, je me lève à sept heures moins le quart. **06h45**

Je prends le petit-déjeuner à sept heures et quart. **07h15**

Je mange une tartine – du pain avec du beurre – et je bois un chocolat chaud.

A la récréation, je mange une pomme comme casse-croûte. **10h15**

A midi, je vais à la cantine pour le déjeuner. **12h00**

Je prends une entrée: des carottes râpées, un plat: une saucisse avec de la purée, un fromage et, comme dessert, une salade de fruits.

L'après-midi, à la récré à trois heures et quart je prends mon goûter. C'est un petit gâteau. **15h15**

Le soir, je prends mon dîner avec ma famille à huit heures. **20h00**

On mange des concombres à la crème, du poulet avec du riz et un fruit en dessert. Je bois de l'eau. Dimanche, lundi et jeudi, je dîne plus tôt que mes parents car je dois aller à l'école le lendemain matin.

L'heure des repas

Get ready

Be a good language detective now and find the right words and phrases to copy carefully next to their English equivalent.

1 breakfast   ______________________

2 as a snack   comme ______________

3 lunch   le ______________

4 my [afternoon] snack   mon ______________

5 I have my evening meal   Je prends ______________________

Let's practise

Select a suitable food or drink from the list to complete each sentence.

du café   du chocolat   des raisins   du poisson   des frites   de la salade

1 Pour le petit déjeuner, je bois du ______________________.

2 Pour le déjeuner, je mange ______________________.

3 Pour le goûter, je mange ______________________.

4 Pour le dîner, je mange ______________________.

Have a go

C'est à toi… It's your turn. If a new French-speaking friend asked you, **'Quel est ton repas préféré?'** (Which is your favourite meal?), how could you answer them? Give as much detail as you can.

1 Mon repas préféré est ______________________.

2 Je prends ______________________.

Teacher's tips

La cantine is the term used for school dinners and where they are served. Most French primary schools don't have a hall like British ones, as there are no assemblies. Fruity fact: **des raisins** in French means grapes. Raisins are dried grapes, so in French they are called **des raisins secs**!

We all need instructions to get on. At Kids Club we play a game like 'Simon says…' that starts 'Jacques a dit…' (Jack said) using French instructions such as:

levez-vous   asseyez-vous   regardez   écoutez   répétez écrivez   chantez   dansez   touchez la chaise

Maybe you play this game at school? If not, suggest it because it's fun and helps you learn!

The verbs here are all imperatives, or bossy verbs, addressed to *you* – **vous** – several people at once, or using the polite form of 'you'. Look at the endings of the verbs. Do you see they all end **–ez**?

Some French recipes include verbs as infinitives. Here are some useful ones: **mesurer** – to measure, **verser** – to pour, **mélanger** – to mix, **battre** – to beat, **ajouter** – to add, **faire cuire** – to cook, **vérifier** – to check, **goûter** – to taste.

Read Louis's favourite pancake recipe and underline all the <u>imperatives</u> (–ez).

Recette de crêpes – Préparation pour quatre personnes

Ingrédients: 4 oeufs, 250 g farine, un demi-litre de lait (500 ml), une pincée de sel.

1. Dans un saladier versez la farine et les oeufs.

2. Puis ajoutez le lait tout en mélangeant avec votre fouet (*whisk*).

3. Ajoutez la pincée de sel et mélangez bien.

4. Laissez reposer la pâte à crêpe pendant une heure.

5. Faites cuire vos crêpes fines à la poêle.

6. Tournez chaque crêpe une fois.

7. Goûtez vos crêpes avec du sucre, de la confiture ou ce que vous voulez.

Draw what you will need to make crêpes like Louis.

Qu'est-ce que je fais maintenant?

Get ready

Louis: Salut! C'est le 2 février, c'est la Chandeleur. Je vais faire les crêpes et je vais allumer les bougies. Qu'est-ce que tu vas faire? Raconte-moi, s'il te plaît.

Pancake Day for Louis, like most French people, is 2 February, which is Candlemas, so people eat their pancakes by candlelight. In Louis's email he says, 'I am going to make pancakes and I am going to light candles. What are you going to do? Please tell me.'

'I am going to do something' is easy to translate into French.

I am going – **Je vais** to do – **faire** → **Je vais faire quelque chose**.

In English, when verbs are used as infinitives, they begin 'to', like to do, to measure, to mix.

Let's practise

A toi… Reply to Louis telling him how you are going to make pancakes too.

Salut Louis!

Je vais faire _____ ______ aussi. D'abord, je v ______ verser _____ ______ et les oeufs dans un saladier. Ensuite, _____ ______ ajouter _____ ______ en mélangeant avec mon fouet. Puis je _____ ______ reposer la pâte à crêpe pendant une _______. Je _______ les faire cuire _____ ______ poêle. Enfin, je vais les ________ avec mes amis.

Have a go

Try to follow Louis's recipe and make crêpes for your family and friends – whatever the date!

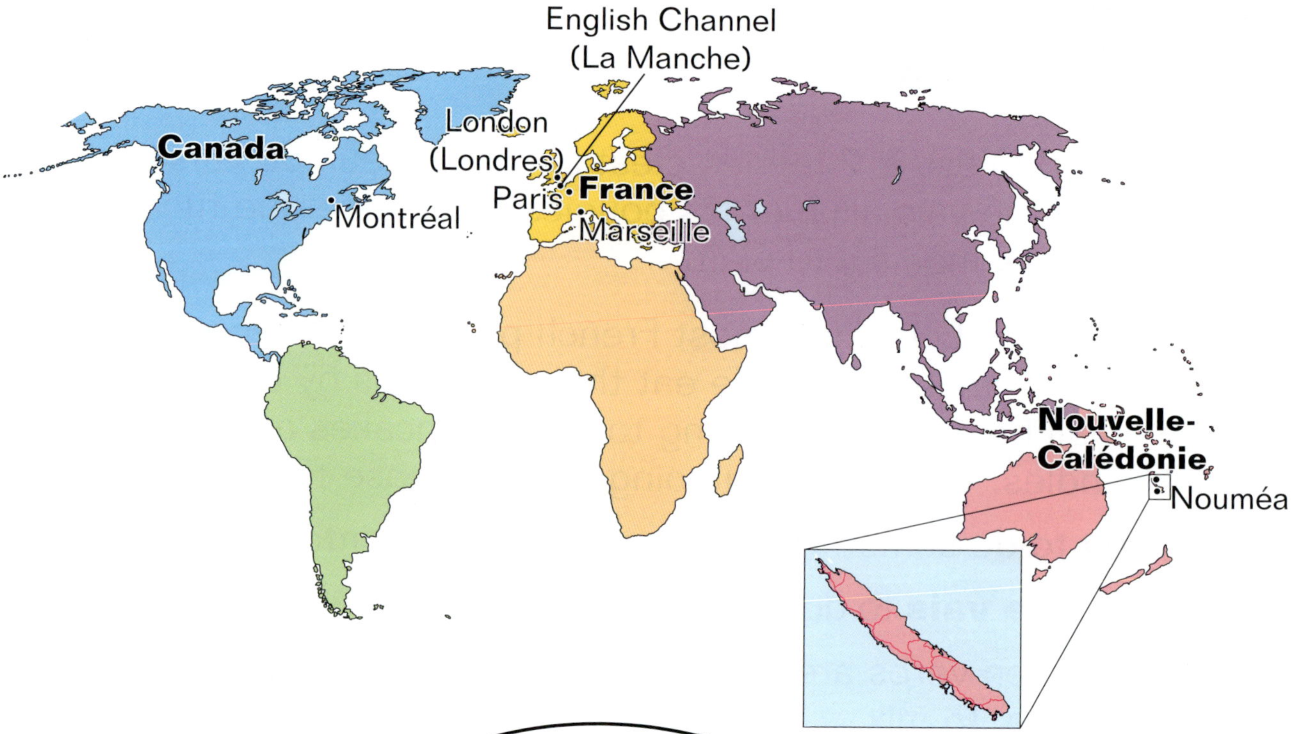

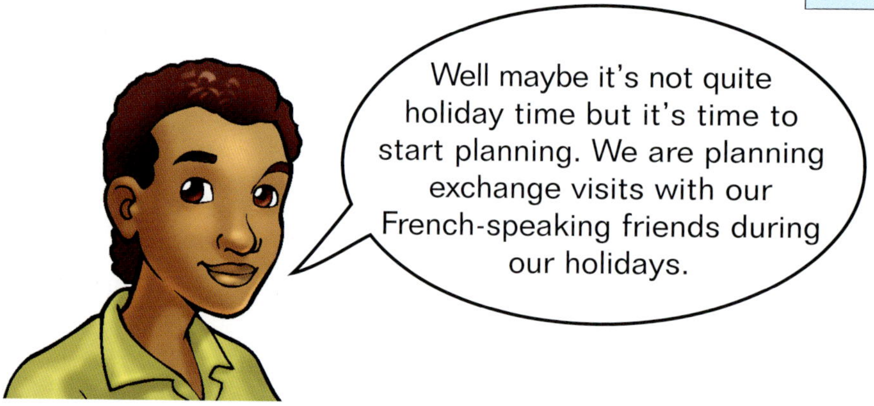

Get ready

Read carefully to find out who is going where and what they are planning to do.

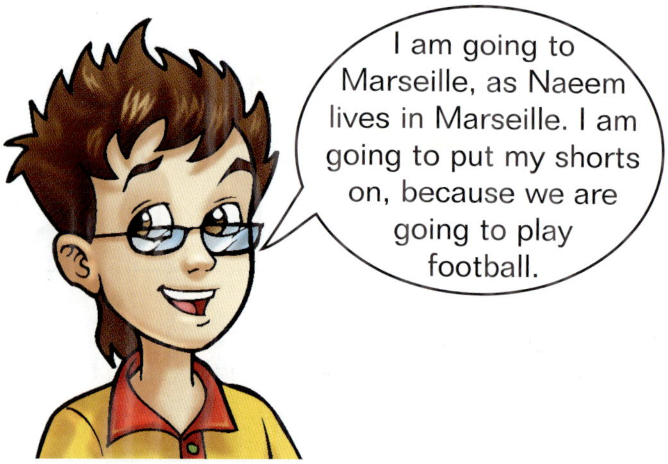

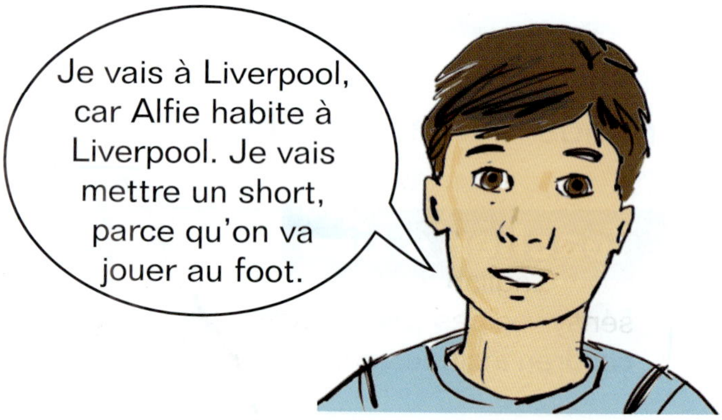

C'est les vacances!

Let's practise

Now read about Mathilde's plans and fill in the gaps.

Have a go

Imagine that you have won a competition to go to visit Louis in New Caledonia or Céline in Canada. Draw a quick portrait of yourself and write about your holiday plans in the speech bubble. Tip: borrow ideas from Naeem and Mathilde, also look back through the book to remind yourself of what else you can include.

How have I done?

	Independently	With support	Not yet
I can ask and answer questions on a variety of topics.	☐	☐	☐
I can read carefully and show that I understand words, phrases and simple text.	☐	☐	☐
I can read poems and rhymes in French.	☐	☐	☐
I can learn new words and know French nouns have a gender. They are masculine (*nm*) or feminine (*nf*).	☐	☐	☐
I can use a dictionary to find new words or to check spellings or definitions.	☐	☐	☐
I understand that verbs change according to the subject of the sentence and I can use a verb table to check.	☐	☐	☐
I can write sentences to express my ideas.	☐	☐	☐
I understand that there are many similarities, as well as many differences, between French and English.	☐	☐	☐

Here are some varied questions and possible answers. Read them carefully and match them up logically. This activity will help you to check how well you have done and justify your answers above.

1. Comment t'appelles-tu?
2. Ça va?
3. Quel âge as-tu?
4. Où habites-tu?
5. Quel temps fait-il?
6. Où sont les lapins?
7. Qu'est-ce que tu vas faire ce soir?
8. Quel est ton plat préféré?

A J'habite à Marseille.

B Mon plat préféré est le curry.

C Les lapins sont dans le jardin.

D Ça va très bien.

E Je m'appelle Isabelle.

F Il y a du soleil.

G J'ai onze ans.

H Je vais faire du vélo ce soir.

Here are answers for each section. In some cases these will be 'suggested answers', as there will be other ways of answering these correctly too.

UNIT 1
Get ready
1 Hello! I am called **Naeem**   **2** Hi! I am **Céline**.   **3** Hello! My name is **Louis**.

Let's practise
1 Salut. **Je** suis Megan.   **2** Mon nom est **Jamelia**.

3 Bonjour, mon nom **est** Kim.   **4** Salutations les lecteurs. Je m'**appelle** Alfie.

UNIT 2
Get ready
Choose any of the phrases listed above the picture of Mathilde.

Have a go
Suggested answer: **Bonjour Naeem. Je m'appelle Kim. Ça va bien. Je suis content de t'écrire par mail.**

UNIT 3
Get ready
1 I am **ten years old**.   **2** I am **eleven years old**.

Let's practise
1 Voici Alfie. **Il a neuf ans**.   **2** Voici Jamelia. **Elle a neuf ans**.   **3** Voici Megan. **Elle a dix ans**.

4 Voici Alfie et Jamelia. Ils ont **neuf ans**.   **5** Voici Megan et Naeem. **Ils ont dix ans**.

Have a go
Suggested answer: **Voici Emily. Elle a dix ans.** You could continue with any phrases you know: **Elle va bien. Elle est sympa. Elle habite à Nottingham. C'est en Angleterre.**

UNIT 4
Let's practise
1 One blue monster.   **2** One red monster and one green monster.

Have a go
The choice is yours.

UNIT 5
Get ready
1 J'**habite**   **2** Il **habite**   **3** Elle **habite**   **4** Il **habite**   **5** Nous **habitons**   **6** Elles **habitent**

Let's practise
Mathilde **habite dans un appartement en ville**.

Naeem **habite dans un appartement au bord de la mer**.

Have a go
Suggested answer: J'habite à Meltham. J'habite dans une maison à la campagne.

UNIT 6
Get ready
1 Le **chien** habite dans une maison à la montagne. Alfie a **un** chien. Il **est** marron.

2 Le lapin **habite** dans un jardin. Elle **a** un lapin. Il **est** noir.

3 La tortue **habite** à la campagne. J'ai une tortue. Elle s'**appelle** Fred.

Let's practise
1 A red dog.   **2** A white rabbit.   **3** A goldfish.   **4** A grey cat   **5** A yellow tortoise.

Have a go
Suggested answer: **J'ai un chien. Il est noir. Il habite avec moi** [with me] **dans une maison à la campagne. Il s'appelle Max. Il a cinq ans.**

UNIT 7
Let's practise
Prepositions are: **1** dans, devant   **2** derrière   **3** sous   **4** dans, à côté de

Have a go
1 Je suis **à** la maison **avec** mon chat.

2 Le chat est **sur** le lit (bed) **dans** ma chambre.

3 Le chien est **dans** le jardin **derrière** la maison. **Devant** or **à côté** de la maison are also correct.

UNIT 8

Get ready

1 Je joue au foot	I play football
2 Je fais du vélo	I ride my bike
3 Je joue au tennis	I play tennis
4 Je fais de la danse	I dance
5 Je fais du skate	I skateboard
6 Je fais de la natation	I swim

Let's practise

1 Charlie: Salut, Abbie! Je joue au foot.

2 Jamelia: Salut, Abbie! Je fais de la danse.

3 Amina: Salut, Abbie! Je joue du piano.

4 Kim: Salut, Abbie! Je joue de la batterie.

UNIT 9

Get ready

1 Je adore le foot.	I love football.
2 J'aime le vélo.	I like riding my bike.
3 Je n'aime pas le tennis.	I don't like tennis.
4 J'aime beaucoup la danse	I like dancing very much.
5 Je n'aime pas du tout le skate.	I don't like skateboarding at all.
6 Je déteste la natation.	I hate swimming.

Let's practise

1 J'aime le sport.	Je n'aime **pas** le **sport**.
2 J'aime la clarinette.	Je **n'**aime **pas** la clarinette.
3 J'aime la musique.	Je n'aime pas **la musique**.

UNIT 10

Get ready

1 Wednesday – Most French primary schools have a four-day week and children do extracurricular activities on Wednesdays. Wednesday afternoon has long been used for this and schools used also to have Saturday morning classes instead.

2 Maths/Numeracy (Mathématique) and French/Literacy (Français).

3 English. English is a foreign language to Mathilde.

4 Twice.

5 Two hours. (Many French children go home for their lunch.)

6 On Thursday mornings she reads in English.

Let's practise

1 Vendredi à 10h30 elle a un cours de Géographie

2 Mercredi elle ne va pas à l'école.

3 Jeudi à 15h30 elle a un cours de Sciences.

4 Mardi et vendredi à 13h30 elle a des cours d'EPS.

Have a go

1 09h00 – Il est **neuf heures**.   **2** 10h30 – Il **est dix heures et demie**.

3 13h30 – Il **est une heure et demie**.   **4** 15h15 – **Il est trois heures et quart**.

5 15h45 – **Il est quatre heures moins le quart**.

UNIT 11

Get ready

1 huit + six = **quatorze**   **2** dix-neuf – quatre = **quinze**   **3** vingt – trois = **dix-sept**   **4** trois x sept = **vingt et un**
5 cinq x cinq = **vingt-cinq**   **6** vingt-sept ÷ neuf = **trois**   **7** trente ÷ six = **cinq**

Let's practise

1 Mon anniversaire c'est le 7 février	07/02
2 Mon anniversaire c'est le 17 mars	17/03
3 Mon anniversaire c'est le 26 juin	26/06
4 Mon anniversaire c'est le 30 août	30/08

UNIT 12
Get ready
1 C'est le 1er avril   Poisson d'avril!

2 C'est le dimanche de Pâques   Joyeuses Pâques

3 C'est le 19 septembre, Sainte Émilie Bonne fête, Émilie!

4 C'est Noël. C'est le 25 décembre.   Joyeux Noël

Have a go
1 Le premier jour du printemps est le **21 mars**.

2 Le premier jour de l'été est le **21 juin**.

3 Le premier jour de l'automne est **le 21 septembre**.

4 Le premier jour de l'hiver est **le 21 décembre**.

UNIT 13
Let's practise
Louis: **1** Il fait 35°C. Il fait **chaud** à Nouméa.

    2 Bonjour Céline! **Quel** temps fait-il à Montréal?

Céline: **3** Il fait −15°C. Il fait très **froid**.

    4 Bonjour Naeem! Quel **temps fait-il** à Marseille?

Naeem: **5** Il fait 26°C. **Il y a** du soleil à Marseille.

Have a go
Suggested answers: **1** Samedi, il fait beau. Il fait 20°C.   **2** Dimanche, il pleut. Il fait 16°C.

UNIT 14
Translation of the song *Promenons-nous dans les bois*:

(Chorus)
Let's go for a walk in the woods,
While the wolf isn't there.
If the wolf was there
He would eat us,
But as he isn't there,
He won't eat us.
Wolf, are you there? What are you doing? Can you hear me?
The wolf: 'I am putting on my shirt.' (Chorus)
The wolf: 'I am putting on my pants.' (Chorus)
The wolf: 'I am putting on my socks.' (Chorus)
The wolf: 'I am putting on my jacket.' (Chorus)
The wolf: 'I am putting on my boots.' (Chorus)
The wolf: 'I am putting on my hat and I am coming.'
Let's run away!

Get ready

1 Shirt	ma chemise	singular	feminine	nf
2 Socks	mes chaussettes	plural	feminine*	npl
3 Hat	mon chapeau	singular	masculine	nm

Mes does not tell you the gender of a plural noun, but you will find that nouns ending in *-ette* are nearly always feminine.

Let's practise
Suggested answers:

1 Quand il fait froid, je mets mes **gants bleus**.

2 Quand il fait mauvais, je mets **mon manteau vert**.

3 Quand il fait chaud, je **mets mon short blanc**.

UNIT 15
Make a list: **épaules, genoux, pieds, yeux, oreilles**.

Let's practise
Your mini-monster should have a red head, green feet, blue eyes, a yellow mouth and an orange nose.

Suggested answer:

Voici mon nouveau mini-monstre. Il s'appelle (**any name you choose**).

Il a **la tête verte***, **les pieds jaunes**, **les yeux rouges**, **la bouche noire et le nez violet**. (*When an adjective that does not usually end in e describes a feminine noun, you need to add an e at the end.)

UNIT 16
Get ready
1 petit-déjeuner   **2** casse-croûte   **3** déjeuner   **4** goûter   **5** mon dîner

Let's practise
Suggested answers:

1 Pour le petit déjeuner, je bois **du chocolat/du café**.

2 Pour le déjeuner, je mange **du poisson/des frites/de la salade**.

3 Pour le goûter, je mange **des raisins**.

4 Pour le dîner, je mange **du poisson/des frites/de la salade**.

Have a go
Suggested answers:

1 Mon repas préféré est **le dîner**.

2 Je prends **du poulet avec des frites et de la salade**.

UNIT 17
The imperatives are:

<u>versez</u>   <u>ajoutez</u> (twice)   <u>mélangez</u>   <u>Laissez</u>   <u>Faites</u>* (*This is the imperative of faire – to do)
<u>Tournez</u>   <u>Goûtez</u>

Note: 'voulez' is not an imperative in the phrase: ou ce que vous voulez.

In the box we should see: e.g. flour, eggs, milk, pinch of salt – sugar, jam.

Let's practise
Salut Louis! Je vais faire **des crêpes** aussi. D'abord, je **vais** verser **la farine** et les oeufs dans un saladier. Ensuite, **je vais** ajouter **le lait** en mélangeant avec mon fouet. Puis je **vais laisser** reposer la pâte à crêpe pendant une **heure**. Je **vais** les faire cuire **à la** poêle. Enfin, je vais les **goûter** avec mes amis.

UNIT 18
Let's practise
'Je vais à Londres, car Jamelia **habite** à Londres. Je **vais** mettre **ma** robe préférée, parce qu'on va faire la fête.'

HOW HAVE I DONE?
1-E, **2**-D, **3**-G, **4**-A, **5**-F, **6**-C, **7**-H, **8**-B. Did you match these up correctly? Bravo!

Language tools

KNOWLEDGE ABOUT LANGUAGE AND LANGUAGE LEARNING STRATEGIES

Spelling, punctuation and grammar

Remember to use what you already know about the English language, from **grammar, punctuation and spelling** learning in school, to help you to learn another language. Of course there are many differences between English and French, such as the gender of nouns, but there are lots of similarities too.

The Romans and French

Etymology explains the roots of the meanings of words – where a word comes from. History tells us that the Romans invaded and settled in France and Britain (and the rest of the Roman Empire of course!), bringing with them their language – Latin. When they left, together with roads, walls, mosaics, etc. they also left their Latin mark on our languages.

This means that many words in French and English have their roots in Latin and look the same or very similar. These are known as **cognates** and include words such as: animal – *animal*, dance – *danse*, trumpet – *trompette*, forest – *forêt*, tortoise – *tortue*. We can also work out links, which help us to remember the meaning of the French word. For example, to live and *habiter* are very different words but we use the word 'habitat' to describe where something lives. It also means we can make good guesses about the meaning of words in French.

Faux-amis or false friends

Unfortunately there is another group of words known as **les faux-amis** or false friends, which resemble each other but do not mean the same thing. Here are a few French words that don't mean what we might expect: *car* – as or because, *veste* – jacket, *raisins* – grapes, *fête* – party, *pain* – bread.

Really important little words

It is easy to overlook short words but we use them all the time. Make sure you learn these:

The – le, la, les

A – un, une

Some – du, de l', de la, des, quelques

Someone – quelqu'un

My – mon, ma, mes

Your – ton, ta, tes

Where – où

When – quand

Which/What – quel, quelle, quels, quelles

What is it? – Qu'est-ce que c'est?

It is/this is – c'est

There is/there are – il y a

There – y, là

Here – ici

In – dans, (en – en France, au – au Canada)

To/at – à

To the – au, à l', à la, aux (pl.)

Et – and

With – avec

Because/as – parce que, car

But – mais

Please – s'il te plaît, s'il vous plaît

Thank you – merci

Yes – oui

No – non

The French word **on** is often used to mean we (or one, if you talk like royalty). It is followed by verbs that are spelled the same way as for il/elle.

Verb tables

You will find verb tables for some frequently used verbs in this book: to have – *avoir* (p. 10), to be – *être* (p. 12) and to live – *habiter* (p. 14). The following verbs are also useful to know.

To go	Aller
I go	Je vais
You go	Tu vas
He goes She goes It goes	Il va Elle va Il va/Elle va – depends on noun gender
We go	Nous allons
You go (*plural or/and respectful*)	Vous allez
They go	Ils vont Elles vont

To do – also To make	Faire
I make	Je fais
You make	Tu fais
He makes She makes It makes	Il fait Elle fait Il fait/Elle fait
We make	Nous faisons
You make (*plural or/and respectful*)	Vous faîtes
They make	Ils font Elles font

NUMBERS
Les nombres

0 zéro	15 quinze	30 trente	72 soixante-douze
1 un/une	16 seize	31 trente et un	73 soixante-treize
2 deux	17 dix-sept	32 trente-deux	74 soixante-quatorze
3 trois	18 dix-huit	33 trente-trois	75 soixante-quinze
4 quatre	19 dix-neuf	34 trente-quatre	76 soixante-seize
5 cinq	20 vingt	35 trente-cinq	77 soixante-dix-sept
6 six	21 vingt et un	36 trente-six	78 soixante-dix-huit
7 sept	22 vingt-deux	37 trente-sept	79 soixante-dix-neuf
8 huit	23 vingt-trois	38 trente-huit	80 quatre-vingts
9 neuf	24 vingt-quatre	39 trente-neuf	81 quatre-vingt-un
10 dix	25 vingt-cinq	40 quarante	82 quatre-vingt-deux
11 onze	26 vingt-six	50 cinquante	90 quatre-vingt-dix
12 douze	27 vingt-sept	60 soixante	91 quatre-vingt-onze
13 treize	28 vingt-huit	70 soixante-dix	99 quatre-vingt-dix-neuf
14 quatorze	29 vingt-neuf	71 soixante et onze	100 cent

TIME

What's the time?   It's…
Quelle heure est-il?   Il est…

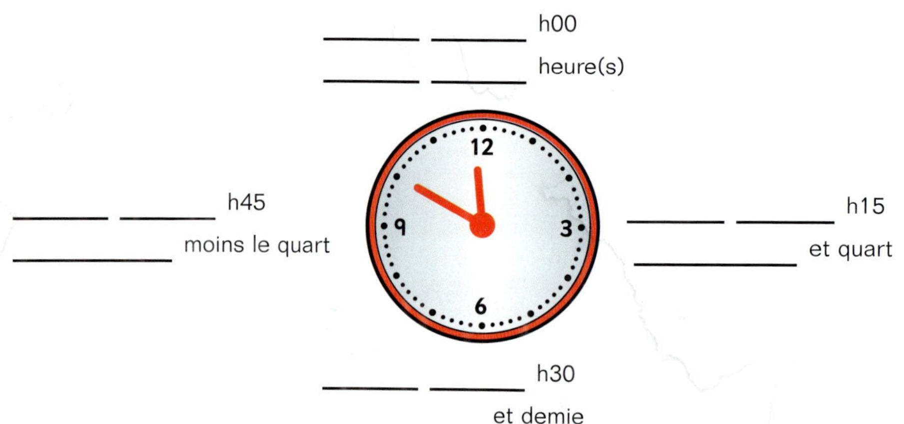